WILDLIFE

Series editor KENNETH BAILEY
Design by WESTPOINT
Cover photograph by courtesy of The Scottish Tourist Board

© SPURBBOOKS 1982
Published by SPURBOOKS (a division of Holmes McDougall Ltd),
Allander House, 137 Leith Walk, Edinburgh EH6 8NS

Printed in Great Britain by Holmes McDougall Ltd, Edinburgh
ISBN 0 7157 2085 6

WILDLIFE

David Stephen

Drawings by Richard Hook

Spurbooks

CONTENTS

INTRODUCTION

SCOTLAND still has a wildlife complex that can compare favourably with any area of similar size in Europe. Since his advent, man has been the main factor in disrupting and changing habitats, and in direct killing out of species. Climatic change has had nothing to do with the extermination of species in the last 2,000 years.

In prehistoric times the giant Irish elk disappeared, probably before it could meet a human being. A magnificent animal, growing a spread of antlers weighing ninety pounds, it is unlikely that the Irish elk would have survived beyond the Pleistocene, so it must be written off as a loss due to failure to adapt to changing conditions. The red deer, on the other hand, survived by the adaptation of reduced body size.

Other losses in prehistoric times were the lemming and northern rat-vole. The lynx, it is reckoned, lasted until man arrived to push it over the edge into oblivion. And from then on man took over as the principal actor in the drama of wildlife extermination.

In historic times Scotland lost the wild ox, the wild boar, the native pony, the brown bear, the reindeer, the elk, the beaver and the wolf. The last survived long enough to become British. The extermination of these species was related in almost every case to the destruction of the forest: the great Forest of Caledon, remnants of which can still be seen at Rannoch and Rothiemurchus.

The modern killing era began in the nineteeth century: the period of the game preserver's ascendancy. It is true that many factors were involved in the destruction of wildlife and habitats: the coming of the sheep; the building of roads and railways; the spread of towns; changed farming practices; the draining of marshes; river pollution; hydro-electric schemes and reafforestation; but the one constant, active factor in wildlife destruction in the nineteenth and twentieth centuries has been the game preserver.

In an age when conservation is alive as a concept, and urgently necessary as a practice, the game preserver is still too often allowed to be the arbiter between life and death.

David Stephen

MAMMALS

RED DEER

THE red deer is the largest land animal in Scotland, and the big battalions, numbering about a quarter of a million, are found in the Highlands and Islands. There are also red deer in the Southern Uplands.

The male red deer is a stag, and stands over four feet at the shoulder; the female, known as a hind, is smaller. Young of either sex are calves, and are spotted with white at birth. The spots disappear in early autumn. The yearling stag, in his first antler spikes, is known as a knobber. A good hill stag will weigh eighteen stone gralloched (that is, gutted), but weight is largely a matter of feeding, and Highland beasts cannot make the antler or body growth of their well nourished park kin.

Stags are known by the number of tines, or points, on their antlers: eight-pointer, ten-pointer, or whatever. A stag with twelve points is a Royal. A balanced fourteen-pointer is an Imperial. Some stags never grow antlers and are known as hummels.

For much of the year – in winter, and when the stags are growing their new antlers – the deer herd mainly by sex: stag groups and hind groups. But there's always some mixing. Young males, called staggies and knobbers, will often be running with hinds. In severe winter conditions, during blizzards or spells of deep snow, the deer are forced to lower ground and then you'll see the groups close together in the same glen.

The red stag casts his old antlers in spring, the strongest beasts losing them first. The new antlers begin to grow almost at once. During the growing period they are covered in a furry overlay known as velvet. In August/September the antlers are fully grown and the stag cleans them of velvet by thrashing in heather or rubbing against trees. For a little while they look ragged – in tatters – with shrivelled lappets quivering in the wind. When they are clean, the stag is ready to take the rut.

The breeding season in red deer is known as the rut, and the old camaraderie among the stags falls apart as the beasts come into peak condition, maned-up, clean-antlered, and with plenty of body fat. From mid-September onwards they leave their groups, in ones or twos or threes, to travel in search of hinds. When a stag breaks into hind ground he announces his arrival with loud roars of challenge, and is ready to fight with any other stag he may meet there.

Red deer are not territorial in the ordinary sense, and rutting stags hold hinds, rather than ground. Each stag collects as big a harem as he can hold, but it is unlikely that any beast can last through the whole rut. The master has little time to eat or sleep; he is kept on the move fighting off intruding stags. So he loses condition quickly, and in the end he is 'run out'. Another stag takes over the group. Then another. And the hinds appear to accept changes of lordship without fuss.

But the senior hind of the group is always the leader, and if she decides to move the others move with her, and the stag has to follow whether he likes it or not. The red deer society is a matriarchy. Hind rule. The stag's monarchy is brief, and constitutional.

After the rut the stags come together again, to feed and recuperate. The groups reform. The rivalries of the rut are forgotten and the old camaraderie is restored. But the stags are out of condition for some time and an early winter can find many of them in poor shape to survive.

The hinds give birth to their calves in June. Single calves are the rule. Hinds are good mothers, and suckle their calves well

Red deer, the largest animal in Scotland

into the winter. The social bonds are strong, and it isn't unusual to find one hind looking after two or three calves while their mothers are grazing some distance away. In summer the deer live high, and it is a pleasant experience to lie out for a night on the high ground, watching the adults grazing and the talkative calves at play.

Outside the calf stage, the red deer has no enemies other than man, who is by far the greatest predator. Young calves may fall prey to eagle or mountain fox, and the eagle is capable of killing a beast several months old, although it is doubtful if this happens very often. Stillborn calves appear to be a rarity, but they do occur, and a hind will tryst with her dead for a day or more before reluctantly leaving it. Then it will be scavenged by, or shared among, fox, eagle, raven, hoodie crow, perhaps even wildcat and badger.

Much has been written, and said, about the fierce fights between rutting stags. In fact fighting is largely formalised, with much threat and bluster, and a great deal of pushing, with victory going to the more powerful pusher. But stags can and do

9

wound each other, although rarely seriously. Infrequently two stags may get their antlers locked. If they can't separate themselves, they will almost certainly die of starvation unless the stalker finds them and saws them apart.

ROE DEER

The roe is the small-antlered deer, the *Boc-earb* of the Gael, and is common and widespread in Scotland. It is usually referred to as a woodland species, as compared with the red deer in its barren, treeless forests. But the red deer was forced to adapt to its spartan existence when its natural habitat – the primeval forest: the great Wood of Caledon – was destroyed. The roe deer has been luckier. There is still plenty of the right kind of habitat for it all over Scotland, even near towns.

Although you're likely to find roe in any kind of cover, they do have their preferences. They like young plantations, birch thickets, mixed woodland, scrubland, or tall forest, near open areas of browse or grazing. They also like birch swamps and reed beds. In winter they like heavy cover to shelter in, and in summer they like plenty of shade.

The male roe deer is a roebuck, never a stag, and he grows antlers, about nine inches long and usually carrying six points. The female is a doe, never a hind, and she doesn't grow antlers, except in rare cases. Young roe of either sex are called kids or fawns. Never calves. An adult roebuck will stand from two feet one inch to two feet five inches at the shoulder, and weigh from thirty-five to sixty pounds. Bucks over sixty pounds aren't common. Does are smaller, weighing from twenty-five to forty pounds when fully grown.

The summer coat of the roe is foxy red; short and tight. In winter it varies through many shades of grey or grey-brown, and is dense and brittle. A white patch on the gullet and another on the throat are characteristic of the roe in winter. The does, young and old, grow a prominent anal tuft that looks like a tail. This isn't found in bucks. Roe deer have no visible tail. The white rump patch is spread open when the deer is alarmed or in flight.

Roe deer are territorial. Within their home range the bucks defend an area, acting aggressively against other bucks, and driving them out if they can. They mark their territorial boundaries by setting scent and fraying vegetation with their antlers. Master bucks also advertise their presence by barking, and the deep *bough* of a mature animal could be mistaken for the barking of a big dog. The home range of the doe overlaps the territory of the buck; indeed it may overlap the territories of two or three males. The home range of several does may overlap the territory of a single buck. Does, before and after the birth of their fawns, will drive out intruding does. Although any buck in any year may be monogamous, the idea that roe pair for life is highly questionable, even unlikely.

With roe deer twin births are normal, although only one fawn may survive. Triplets occur from time to time, and some does manage to rear them. This has nothing to do with a doe adopting a motherless fawn, as sometimes happens. At birth the fawns are spotted with white. The spots fade out in early autumn. Fawns are born in late May, into June.

Buck fawns, depending on their date of birth, grow hard, horny buttons on their pedicles in November or December, and lose them in January or February. After that the first real antlers begin to sprout, on the pedicles. The pedicles are the protuberances from the skull, on which the antlers grow, and which produce the bone-forming material of which they are made. The fawn's first antlers, unlike the buttons, are covered in velvet, which is rubbed off in late spring. These first antlers may be, and often are, single spikes; but they may also fork, giving a four-point head. A well nourished youngster, on good ground, may put up six points in his first year.

Adult bucks cast their old antlers in November/December, and clean their new ones in March/April. Young bucks cast later.

The rut is in July and August. The bucks become highly excited and active — barking, grunting, fraying vegetation and 'attacking' branches of trees, setting scent, and scraping the

The roe is the small-antlered deer

ground in the rutting area with their hooves. When two bucks meet fighting can be fierce. Wounding, especially on the flanks, is common but superficial; sometimes it can be more serious. One buck may even kill another, but this must be very rare. I have seen it happen only once in my life.

A master buck will run his doe in a circle: ringing as it is commonly called. He will run her in this fashion until he is out of breath, and mate her on the ring. These so-called fairy rings of the roe are perfectly obvious to the kenning eye, and almost invariably are round some prominent central object: a tree, a rock or a clump of heather or blaeberry. They are used at other times, but nobody really knows what they are all about.

Although the rut takes place much earlier than in the red deer, the young are born about the same time the following year, which would seem to make the gestation period of the roe longer than that of the red. This is because of delayed implantation. After fertilisation the eggs grow to the blastocyst stage. The blastocysts remain free in the uterus until December or January, when they become implanted in the uterine wall. Then real development begins, and the young are born five or six months later. The roe is the only deer in which there is delayed implantation.

Roe deer are active at nightfall and dawn, but in quiet places can be seen on foot during the day. They are browsers and grazers and eat a wide variety of wild plants. On the hill they eat heather as well as grass. Juniper is an important food plant in some areas during the winter.

The dog-like bark is probably the roe's best known vocal display. Bucks also grunt like pigs. The doe has a *whee-yoo* call to her fawns. Their answer is a call like *eep-eep-nee-eep*. A fawn in distress, or when taken by a predator, cries like a hare. Apart from man, the main predators on roe fawns are the eagle, the fox, roving dogs and, less commonly, the wildcat.

SIKA DEER

Sika deer are found in Argyll, Caithness, Inverness, Ross and Sutherland. Several races of this deer have been introduced, but the one that has proved most viable is the Japanese, and this is the type found in Scotland.

Compared with the red deer, for which it can quite readily be mistaken, the Sika looks puckered, down in front and behind, which gives it a skulking appearance. Although it is smaller than the red deer, size doesn't indicate much if you don't see them together. Nor does colour. One striking difference is in the stag's antler velvet. This is red, tipped with black. The antlers are in the velvet from May to August.

In summer coat the sika is as red as the roe: the winter coat is much darker. The calves are spotted at birth. The tail of the sika is white; the rump patch white edged with black. Like red deer stags, the sika stags are polygamous. The rut is in October into November, when the sika stag whistles: a sound uttered by no other British deer.

Sika are deer of the forest edge, so are most likely to be seen

13

near woodlands. They like plenty of thicket cover, especially hazel, bracken and bramble; but they will also be found lying up in deep heather, clumps of unbrashed conifers, or in birch or alder swamps. On the hill they eat the same food as the red deer. They are fond of the shoots and bark of hazel.

It isn't unusual to see sika grouped by sex as in red deer, but it isn't usual to see them in large herds, however numerous they may be on the ground.

FALLOW DEER

To a great many people the fallow deer is a tame park animal, and to a great extent they're right. Many feral fallow in Scotland behave with a great degree of tolerance towards human beings. Others are much shyer, and some are as wild and wary as the red deer or the roe.

Fallow deer prefer deciduous woodland, although they will sometimes be found sharing the same ground as red deer. On open ground they will lie up in bracken, and regularly drop their fawns there. Finding them in thick woodland can be difficult; stalking them there even more so. Wise old bucks will lie up in thick cover all day, and feed only at nightfall and dawn.

A mature fallow buck will stand under or over three feet at the shoulder. A good buck will scale fifteen stone. Does are smaller and lighter. Only the bucks grow antlers, which are palmate, broadening with maturity. The antlers are cast in April or May, and the new ones clean in late August into September.

The rut is in October, and lasts into early November, by which time all the excitement is over. Each master buck defends his rutting area against all comers, but serious fighting is rare. There is an order of precedence among bucks, which is observed with some strictness until a younger beast feels like challenging. Then there will be a fight. But most fights are little more than threat displays. But when a real challenger comes along the master may be toppled after a severe battle.

After the rut fallow herd mainly by sex. The does leave to give birth to their fawns, then come together again. At birth the fawns are spotted — with white in the pale varieties, indistinctly in the dark varieties. The fawns are very playful, and the does spend a great deal of time with them when they're small, skipping this way and that, running in circles, and bounding stiff-legged to twice their height.

REINDEER

The native reindeer of Scotland became extinct in the twelfth century. Many centuries passed before any attempt was made to introduce them. Fourteen animals were brought to Dunkeld by the Duke of Atholl in the eighteenth century, all of which died, the longest lived surviving for not more than two years. Other reintroductions were tried in Mar Forest and in Orkney, but without success. It was left for Mikel Utsi to reintroduce them successfully from Sweden in 1952.

Mikel Utsi is dead, but the descendants of his reindeer live on in the Cairngorms near Rothiemurchus. His first animals were of the mountain type; later he brought in the woodland type, the one considered to be that formerly found in Scotland. Since then the herd has been breeding successfully, and is, apart from anything else, a great tourist attraction.

Reindeer in Scandinavia and North America feed mainly on a lichen known as reindeer moss. They eat this in Scotland too, but they take other food as well. Male reindeer are known as bulls; females are cows. Calves are born in May and June, and are unspotted. The reindeer is the only species in which both sexes have antlers.

WILD GOAT

There are no wild goats in Scotland in the strict sense: only domestic goats living wild. Although the present herds are wild 15 enough, some of them as difficult to stalk as the wildest red deer on the hill, they are all the descendants of former domestic animals. It is a tendency with goats to run wild, and a lot of them did so in Scotland many centuries ago. One of the herds with an ancient lineage is that on Ben Lomond, which is thought to have been there since the time of Robert Bruce. Almost, but not quite, all of today's herds are in the west, the north-west and the Southern Uplands.

Feral goats in Scotland come in a variety of colours and markings: black-and-white, brown-and-white, black, brown, white and even cream. Kids are often beautifully coloured. Adult billies grow horns like the true wild goat, their ancestor from Persia.

Depending on human pressure, wild goats show great variation in their behaviour towards human beings. Where they are not greatly disturbed, or shot at, they will tolerate people within a hundred yards. But on ground where they are much disturbed and harried they can be truly wild and unapproachable. When under such pressure they will cling to the high tops and the wildest screes.

Goats move about in small herds, and up and down through the contours. When alarmed they give an explosive hiss that can be heard a long way off. Red deer know what this hiss means and react accordingly. Thus the goat acts as the eyes and ears of the deer before the deer have time to use their own.

The mating season is in October and November, when there is fighting among the billies. Head to head encounters are common but appear to cause little damage. A nanny with a kid will fight off a billy, engaging him horn to horn. Kids are born in the period February/March, when the weather can be most severe. Mortality among kids can be high. Early births, and a harsh environment, mean rigorous selection.

Man is the main predator on the wild goat, which has been exterminated in some areas by the Forestry Commission, because of damage done to trees. The goat kid is within the prey range of the eagle and the fox for about the same time as the hill lamb. But nanny goats can be bold in defence of their young, and some will attack fox or dog on sight. They have no defence

16

against the eagle, whose predation is almost certainly insignificant.

SOAY SHEEP

The Soay sheep is an ancient breed, which has lived on the St Kilda group of islands in association with man for a thousand years and more, and may even have been there before the Viking conquest. The islands of Soay, Dun and Hirta are its ancestral home. The breed has remained pure, despite the introduction of other types, and no other sheep like it exists today.

The breed exists in two colour phases: the dark brown type, almost black in autumn but lighter in spring, and the less common light brown type. Although it closely resembles the wild moufflon in many ways (horns, throat hair and mane) it is a much smaller beast. The adult fleece is fine soft wool mixed with hair.

The St Kildans harvested the Soay, but they had to hunt it like a wild animal, as it will not submit to orthodox dogging. A party of scientists once tried to herd them with a well-trained mainland sheepdog, without success. The St Kildans trained their own dogs to drive them into dead ends where they could be caught.

The food of the Soay is grass and maritime vegetation. Most of the present-day stock run at sight of a human being, but the animals grazing about the old village have become familiar with the new residents and tolerate them to within ten yards. Since 1955 the Hirta flocks have been counted annually, and each year about one in ten of the population has been caught, measured and tagged. The census has shown that there is a population fluctuation on a definite cycle.

Soays breed in October, and lambs are born in March and April. Many ewes become pregnant in their first winter, and many rams of the year will breed in their first October.

Nowadays Soays can be seen in a number of parks on the 17

mainland, in places as different as Aviemore and Cumbernauld, and small units of the breed have been introduced to other islands.

OTTER

The otter is the sleek weasel of the water: sinuous, steamlined like a seal, apparently boneless as he dives, swims, twists, or rolls on the surface. When he runs on land he has the hump-backed appearance of all the weasels; in the water or out of it he can do nothing gracelessly. Web-footed, and with a tail that is a powerful rudder, he is supremely adapted for life in the water: yet he has not become an over-specialised hunter, and can be a land weasel when he has to, or wants to.

Otters hunt mainly at night, except when food is scarce. When there's snow on the ground, the beast leaves a plain trail with a distinctive signature. Such trails may lead over many miles of country, far from river or burn. In the Highlands, you'll find tracks going right over the mountains tops, from one glen to another, in mid-winter.

Tracks may lead to a rabbit warren, or to a farmhouse, for the otter takes rabbits, mice, voles, and anything he can find. When faced with famine he will take poultry, ducks, and even turkeys. But such happenings are the exception.

It is as a fisherman that the otter excels; it is the role for which he is so well designed. Like the seal he has the powerful ear and nose muscles that snap shut before a dive; and a heavy bush of sensitive whiskers set in his swollen upper lip.

Swimming under water comes as easily to him as running overland. Whatever else they may eat, the main food of otters is fish: game fish, coarse fish, eels, freshwater crayfish, crabs, other crustaceans, mussels, and probably saithe, lythe, and other rock fish.

It is charged against the otter that he reduces the stock of game fish. This has never been demonstrated, and modern research on predation indicates that it is highly questionable. If

The otter is the sleek weasel of the water

game fish ever became scare it will not be because of predation by otters; where such fish have become scarce the cause is usually pollution, which affects the otter in the same way and to the same extent. The otters of the Western Isles of Scotland spend much of their time in the sea, where they prey on marine life, including shellfish.

Much has been made of the otter's so-called wastefulness: the old one about the beast taking a bite out of the shoulder of a big fish and leaving the rest. Like other members of the weasel family he can be choosey when prey is abundant; but when it is scarce, or hard to come by, he will eat every scrap that can be eaten. In the life cycle of the salmon the otter is probably the least significant predator. An otter in a hatchery is something else. There he can do much damage, and has to be dealt with accordingly, as an individual.

Sporting man is all too prone to look upon anything killing the same prey as himself as a competitor, which doesn't follow at all: he is even more prone to assume that other predators are as wasteful as he.

19

The otter has become known as the great wanderer, travelling down to the sea, from rivermouth to watershed, and from one river to another. The reason for these wanderings is not yet fully understood. Otter hunters used to find the beasts spread out evenly along the best river habitats at intervals of about five miles. The impression one gets along the rocky sea coast of Wester Ross and the Western Isles is an even distribution at intervals of several miles along the best river habitats. If, as it seems, the otter is territorial like other mustelids, these wanderers could be mainly dispersing juveniles, or transient adults in search of a range of their own.

There is no fixed breeding season: cubs are born in any month of the year. This is the settled time for otters, for the dog stays with the bitch at least until after the cubs are weaned, and she will not move until they are swimming strongly and able to hunt for themselves. On Mull, dog and bitch have been seen with well-grown cubs, all living and playing together. The dog otter usually lies downstream from the holt, and will fight with any other dog that tries to move up past him. The belief that he develops a wanderlust after the cubs are weaned has never been substantiated.

Although cubs have an inborn ability to swim, and do so from the moment they're in the water, they often show a marked reluctance to take the first plunge, and have sometimes to be cajoled or pushed into it.

The otter has now been given the same protection in Scotland as in England, where it has become extremely rare. It has become rare over much of Scotland, too, and there is no doubt that pollution and disturbance are factors in this decline. Today the beast's strongholds are in the west and north-west, and the Western and Northern Isles.

BADGER

The badger has been called the last of the British bears. In fact he's a true weasel. The bear-like badger ceases to exist as soon as he begins to move. Then he's all weasel, with the rippling run typical of the clan.

Although stoutly built – sheathed in muscle, big clawed, hand-footed and out at elbow, strong jawed, broad chested, squat and bear-like – he is neither slow nor plodding. He can be as quick off his mark as any weasel. He hasn't the speed to course a full grown rabbit in the open, but he's fast enough over a short spurt to catch a young one. You have only to watch an alarmed brock rushing back to his set to realise how quickly he can move when he has to.

Any terrier that has faced a badger knows just how quickly the brock can turn his head to bring his jaws into action. And what jaws they are, capable of breaking a terrier's jaw, killing a fox, or taking the fingers off your hand. But the brock is a quiet, pacific beast when left alone, and brings his jaws, as weaponry, into action only when the turned cheek and the peace conference have failed.

It's strange that this beast, one of the cleanest of mammals, should so often have the epithet dirty applied to him. His reputation for cleanliness arises from his housekeeping and his personal habits. He is meticulously clean in himself (give or take his fleas); he keeps his den clean; and outside it he digs his latrines. When he finishes with one he scrapes earth over it and digs a new one. The presence of such latrines is one indication of the presence of badgers in a set.

A badger's den is called a set, and the holes are easily distinguished from rabbit burrows, whether they've been worked on by a fox or not. The vixen who enlarges a rabbit burrow as a nursery is content to dig out one hole, and scrape out just enough sand or earth as is absolutely necessary. She drags in no bedding of any kind, whereas the badger drags in quantities of hay and bracken and leaves. And the badger goes on digging and digging, with the result of his labours plain for all to see.

A well established badger set becomes a system of tunnels, with massive earthworks fronting each entrance, so that the whole looks like a series of small quarries. The holes are bigger than any fox or rabbit would ever try to dig. You realize just how big and strong a badger is (twice the weight of a big fox) when you see the size of the rocks he brings up during the digging, and the way he can push them about.

In the tunnel system (and there may be two storeys) the badgers have their sleeping nests and breeding nests, all well-padded comfortable beds, frequently aired or renewed. Dead members of the family are walled in off the tunnels, although my old friend, the late Brian Vesey Fitzgerald, once recorded a badger funeral in the open, which goes to show that you can never be sure of anything. But underground burials are the norm, as you can see where badgers begin digging again in a part of the set that has been sealed off for a time. Then the old skulls and bones appear on the surface.

In a big, well established set badgers will leave sections unused for some time, perhaps for as long as two years, and it is in such sections that vixens sometimes settle to rear a family. When you find a fox denned in a badger set she will almost certainly be in such a disused part, and if she pushes through into the occupied part she is liable to be in trouble. The brocks don't seem to bother so long as the fox keeps herself to herself. I've known brocks kill fox cubs in such a situation, and I knew one old boar badger who killed a vixen trapped on his doorstep. This doesn't mean that badgers make a habit of killing foxes. They don't.

Badger cubs are born in January or February, and into March. February/March is more usual for Scotland, especially in the Highlands. Two or three cubs are usual. At the age of eight weeks they begin to explore around the set, and make short forays. Thereafter they make longer and longer journeys, and at the age of four months they know their local geography and are able to fend for themselves.

Mating takes place in spring, shortly after the birth of the cubs. When the sow comes in season the boar makes a great fuss of her, purring like a very strong-purred cat. Matings also take place later, into early autumn. But whatever the time of mating, births take place about the same time in spring. This is because there is delayed implantation in the badger, as in the roe deer and the stoat. Implantation takes place at the end of the year, or in January, and the cubs are born in February/March.

Badgers don't hibernate, but in winter they become less active, especially from late November to January. They'll come out, but they don't go anywhere, unless the night is fine. They like to gorge then lie up for a few days. They'll do this in summer and autumn as well, especially during spells of driving rain or gales. They prefer to come out after sunset, and be home before sunrise, but in quiet places, where they're not disturbed, you'll find them coming out in good light, although they won't go very far until darkening.

The badger although sturdily built is a true weasel

Mountain badgers den high, at 1,500 feet or higher, and you'll find them travelling through the contours, even in winter. Their food varies to some extent according to area; but all brocks eat a lot of earthworms, and all eat vegetable matter. A badger will eat almost anything he can catch and hold. All of them will dig out rabbit nests and eat the young, and all of them will dig out wasp nests and bumble bee bikes.

STOAT AND WEASEL

The weasel is easily recognised, and the stoat is totally different. That old bit of doggerel is perfectly true, but it tells us nothing about either. The two go together in people's minds like ducks and drakes; yet most still seem to have difficulty with which is which.

The stoat is a much bigger beast, about the size of an average bitch ferret. A big dog stoat will measure a foot from the tip of his nose to the root of his tail, which is about four and a half inches long, tapers towards the body, and is bushy with a black tip. Dog stoats are about half as heavy again as bitch stoats. Weight, varying with age and sex, ranges from four ounces in the young up to eleven or twelve ounces in adult males, sometimes even more.

In Scotland dog weasels range from three and a half to seven ounces in weight; females from two to three ounces. But I've weighed bitches at three and a half ounces, and one male at nine ounces, which is pushing hard on the weight of the best stoats. The length of male weasels is from seven to nine inches; females from six and a half to seven and three-quarter inches. These lengths are exclusive of tail, which is a short, smooth tag with no black tip.

Scottish stoats as a rule turn white in winter, when they become ermines. White weasels are extremely rare, although the change is normal in more northerly parts of their range. Some stoats will make only a partial change, and in certain winters some animals don't change at all.

There's no sure way of sexing free animals in the field, although big dog weasels present no real problem to anyone familiar with the species. Even in a family party of stoats the female isn't obvious, because the kits so quickly catch up with her in size; but the biggest beast will certainly be the male. Young weasels also make rapid growth, and male kits at eight weeks are as big as their mother.

In the stoat there is delayed implantation; in the weasel there is not. So stoats breed only once a year. The mating season is in July, with kits born in April or May of the following year. The weasel also has her kits in spring, but more often than not she will have a second in the summer. Some bitches even manage a third litter, but for this to happen conditions have to be optimum. Litter size in the stoat is about the same as in the weasel: six to nine kits.

Weasels suckle their young for three weeks and a bit; stoats for five to six weeks. Male stoats are fertile from March to July, or thereabouts, and in this period all stoats are mated, including young females of the year. There is a record of a young female pregnant at the age of two months. There is no evidence that female weasels breed in their first year.

There is clear evidence that dog stoats help the bitch with the rearing of the family, and that the sexes live together amicably at all times.

Both species are territorial, marking their boundaries by scats, urine and body scent. The males defend these territories against others of their kind, but not against the other species. So you will find stoat and weasel holding and hunting the same ground at the same time, although it is unlikely that their territorial boundaries will be the same.

Both species hold their territory for as long as they can defend it, or until they give it up for some other reason. When Jim Lockie removed a male from his fifty-acre territory in a young forest three males on the perimeter took over the ground at once, each adding about fifteen acres to his territory. I've found exactly the same thing with weasels. Death, failure of food supply, or eviction by a stronger animal, probably account for all territorial changes.

Stoats range through the contours: from sea level to the high tops. They are found high on Ben Nevis, and even in winter may be seen on the same ground as the ptarmigan. Woodland, young plantations, rabbit warrens, agricultural land and sand dunes are typical habitats. Even on the treeless deer forests the beast can find ample cover among heather, rocks and screes.

Weasels occupy much the same kind of ground as the stoat, but are not so often found on mountains or high moorland. Lowland farming country suits them, and they're most likely to be seen in hedgebottoms and on the woodland fringe. Where field voles are plentiful the two will frequently be found together.

Although the two take the same kind of food at the low end of the prey range, the stoat can kill much bigger animals. It will kill anything it can catch and hold: voles of any kind, woodmice, rabbits, leverets, rats, and a variety of birds. On the hill it will take red grouse, black grouse, golden plover and ptarmigan. On low ground it will take partridge and pheasant as opportunity offers. Before myxomatosis the rabbit was a staple prey of many stoats. A stoat requires about a quarter of its body weight in food each day: a dog the equivalent of three field voles, and a bitch the equivalent of two.

The weasel is a specialist predator on voles and mice, especially on field voles which often make up the entire prey for long periods. They also kill young rats, but it takes a very powerful dog weasel to handle a rat of any size in the open. A big rat is quite capable of killing a small weasel. Prey is killed by a bite on the neck (as in the stoat) and is held with the forepaws while being scratched by the hindfeet. Like stoats, weasels eat about a quarter of their body weight a day: dogs about one and a quarter ounces and bitches about an ounce.

The bitch stoat makes her breeding nest in a rabbit burrow, or under the roots of a tree, or in a drystane dyke. I once found one in an old wasp bike. She carries in hay and other herbage, but adds to this, as time goes on, the skins of prey animals so that the nest becomes a ball of mixed fur and hay. The bitch weasel does the same. Both species have their latrine nearby, often on the doorstep, and to this the young will crawl as soon as they are able. Such latrines betray the nest to an observant human eye.

Man is the most important predator on stoats and weasels and, next to him, probably terriers and foxes. Foxes kill either at any time (although some foxes back off when faced up to) but eat them only sometimes, probably when the alternatives are rank mustelid or hunger. Cats kill weasels, and sometimes stoats, but don't eat them. Eagles and buzzard kill, and eat. Weasels, and small stoats, are taken by owls and kestrels from time to time.

The stoat is an expert tracker. Like the weasel, it frequently sits tall, in listening attitude when hunting. Both will hunt in burrows, but the stoat needs more elbow room, and can't follow field voles below ground as the weasel can. When it comes to field voles the stoat has to catch them above ground, or in their surface creep. For this reason the weasel can outlast the stoat on ground where vole numbers are dropping, as they do at the end of a population cycle. The weasel will use mole tunnels to get across a patch of open ground without surfacing.

Both species have been badly served by their publicists. You'd think they were a pair of ravening vampires. They're not. They don't suck blood. Like any other carnivore they kill what they need most of the time. When prey is abundant they will kill more, eating only the choicest parts. Both store surplus food, and remember where they've stored it. If they need it they'll go back for it; if they don't they won't.

Of course they can be fierce if too closely molested, which is what you'd expect. If you poke your nose into a weasel's nursery you're liable to pull back with a firecracker of a weasel on the end of it. A nest of young stoats, with their eyes open, is like a tangle of electrified barbed wire. If you insist on poking your hand in, you'll be bitten. And why not?

PINE MARTEN

At the beginning of the twentieth century the pine marten had been reduced to a remnant population in the north-west. In recent years it has been increasing, mostly north of the Great Glen but also south and east of it, colonising new forests planted by The Forestry Commission and private landowners.

Although naturally an animal of mature pine forest the marten has shown itself to be highly adaptable. When the felling of the great forests, followed by intensive game preservation, forced it into the wildest country of rock and scree, often treeless, it survived into the present century, when tree planting on a vast scale tipped the balance in its favour again.

The marten is the weasel of the trees, and a big one: up to two

27

The pine marten is naturally an animal of the forest

feet nine inches from nose to tail tip. Females are smaller: up to two and a half feet from tip to tip. Weight ranges from two to nearly three and a half pounds. The fur varies in colour from pale chestnut to near black. The round ears have a pale edge, and there is a creamy white patch of variable size on the throat. The winter coat, which grows in during September/October, is thicker than in summer, and the throat patch becomes more orange.

In the Highlands the pine marten preys mainly on small mammals and small birds, the field vole being by far the most common item. Tits, wrens and tree creepers make up most of the bird prey. Beetles, caterpillars, wasp grubs, fish, deer carrion and berries are also eaten. The marten is capable of killing game, but the extent of such predation is not known, and can be nothing but insignificant. It was the game preserver who persecuted it almost out of existence.

There is delayed implantation in this species. The young, averaging three in a litter, are born in late March or early April.

Dens can be in any suitable site: but most are in cairns, holes in trees, or old birds' nests, including the nest of the golden eagle.

The marten is most active from dusk to dawn, but will hunt at all hours when it has to. Most sightings are made at night, often in car headlamps. The beast moves fast, and is a good jumper. A leap of six feet is easy for it, and more than double that distance has been recorded downhill.

Settled males hold territories, into which females are accepted in the breeding season. Dispersing young seem to have one aim: to put as much distance between themselves and their birthplace as possible. The young disperse when they are five to six months old. Resident animals set scent from their abdominal glands on rocks, stumps and branches, thus marking boundaries and bringing the sexes into contact with each other.

WILDCAT

There is no scarcity of wildcats in Scotland today. It has been reviving, and spreading, since its near extinction at the beginning of the century, and is now breeding within fifteen miles of Glasgow (in Stirlingshire). It is now found in all Highland counties.

The popular impression of the wildcat is of a bristling, snarling, spitting fury, with teeth bared to the gums and ears flattened against its skull. It can do all of these things, and add fire and brimstone, but in the ordinary way it goes around like any ordinary cat, with its ears up and its teeth locked away.

Its reputation for untameability is nearer the truth, for this is virtually impossible after the kittens have had their eyes open for a day or two.

The true wildcat is a species. A gone-wild domestic cat can never become a wildcat, however long it may lead the free, wild life. Nor can its offspring. Such kittens may grow to a great size; they will be fierce; but they will not be wildcats. Some domestic cats can make greater weights than true wildcats; but in general the wildcat is bigger and heavier, marked with stripes instead of stripes and blotches. A big male wildcat will measure over three feet from nose to tail tip, the body being fully two feet long. Weight ranges from seven to thirteen pounds or more.

The tail of the wildcat is bushy, clearly ringed, and blunt-ended, the tip being black. The tail of the domestic cat tapers towards the tip. The rings on the tail are less clearly defined and more numerous.

Although primarily a forest animal the wildcat survived in Scotland through being adaptable, contriving to exist on wild, rocky treeless terrain. Nowadays it is found in mature forest and young plantations, as well as on heather moorland and high barren ground.

The den is usually in a cairn or under the roots of a tree; sometimes in the disused eyrie of a golden eagle. Breeding begins in March, and two or three kittens are born in the first half of May. The female rears the kittens, which begin to play about the den mouth at the age of four or five weeks. After that they begin to follow her on hunting forays. Like the mountain fox the cat will move her kittens to a new den if she is disturbed, or for other reasons of her own.

It has been argued that Scottish wildcats breed twice in the year, because young kittens have been found from May to August. It has also been suggested that this is the result of the admixture of domestic blood that takes place from time to time in some areas. It is just as likely, perhaps more likely, that the wildcat, like the otter, has no fixed breeding season.

The wild tom defends a territory and marks it with scats of urine. Wildcats don't bury their droppings. He has places where he sharpens his claws, on trees or rocks as the case may be, and he may set scent at the same time from the glands in his feet.

The prey range is wide; from insects to roe deer fawns. Voles are a favourite item. Other prey includes small birds, birds up to the size of red and black grouse, hares and rabbits, and sometimes fish. The beast is fit to tackle prey the size of a capercaillie. In young plantations voles are the staple diet, with rabbits next on the list.

Man is the only predator on the wildcat, if we except the golden eagle that takes the occasional kitten, and the mountain

There is no scarcity of wildcats in Scotland today

fox that may chop a whole litter. Disputes between eagles and mature wildcats, or between the fox and the wildcat, are usually over food. Normally these species keep out of each other's way.

FOX

The fox is an adaptable and viable species and, given cover and food supply, will live almost anywhere, including towns. Despite constant persecution, often by illegal methods, all the evidence indicates that foxes are as numerous as ever, and likely to hold more than their own.

Besides being a true carnivore, the fox is also a scavenger that will eat almost any kind of carrion: deer, sheep, goats and the contents of litter bins in towns. It kills animals ranging in size from red deer calves to beetles: it takes fruit, some other vegetable matter, and the dead and wounded left by careless shooting men. On the hill it will get through the winter on winter's casualties: dead deer and sheep. In the stalking season it eats the grallochs of stags and hinds.

With a beast of such wide tastes it is difficult and dangerous to generalise about food. It might be said that in lowland areas its main prey is made up of rabbits, voles, rats, mice, game birds, insects, earthworms and roe deer fawns, while on high ground its staples are rabbit, vole, hare, grouse, carrion (a big item), lambs (dead or alive) and red deer calves. A mature fox requires about a pound of food per day.

The golden eagle sometimes kills and eats fox cubs at the age when they are playing about the den mouth. But man is the chief predator, using traps, snares, gas, poison, gunshot and dogs to kill them. In Scotland it isn't a crime to shoot a fox; it is a crime not to shoot one. Almost all fox destruction (euphemistically termed 'control') is based on its predation on lambs. Poultry don't matter nowadays, because most are kept intensively, and the average modern fox would hardly recognise a hen if he saw one. That goes for a lot of people too.

Foxes take dead lambs as everybody knows. Everybody also knows that some foxes kill lambs, and that lambs are killed in some areas and not in others. But nobody knows just how many lambs they kill or in what circumstances. Available evidence suggests that foxes eat more lambs on poor sheep ground, and in years of poor lambing, than on good sheep ground. During fifty-one days on a good sheep hill I found that neither the foxes nor the eagles touched lambs at all.

From the turn of the year onwards foxes are most vocal, for this is the breeding season. The vixen chooses the den – a rabbit burrow, under a tree root, in the disused part of a badger set, or among rocks. Highland foxes often den in screes. Cubs number from four to six, or seven. Occasionally two vixens will den up together. The cubs weigh under four ounces at birth, and are black. At the age of three to four weeks they begin to appear at the den mouth; at six weeks they are strong and boisterous, and at eight weeks they are weaned. But they are eating flesh for some time before then.

A vixen, disturbed, will move her litter. She will do so even when not disturbed, sometimes kennelling them above ground, in good cover, and sometimes splitting the family, as wolves do. The breakup of the family takes place when the cubs are three months old, or a bit more. Both parents provide food, although to begin with, and for some time, the vixen spends most of her time with the cubs. Dog foxes, like dog wolves, are good fathers.

A big vixen, defending cubs, can be a terrible handful for even the toughest terriers sent down to bolt her. In a teeth-to-teeth girning match many a varminty terrier is bitten through the face and scarred for life. Big cubs will grapple with the terrier that is worrying them. But in the end man wins. The vixen is shot as she bolts, then the terriers kill the cubs. That is the Highland way and, if foxes have to be killed, it is probably the best, for it is brief, bloody and final.

POLECAT

In any part of Scotland one is liable to come across a polecat ferret running wild; but it won't be a true polecat, because the true polecat is considered extinct. The polecats on the Isle of Mull are the descendants of ferrets introduced there a long time ago to kill rabbits, so they are not the genuine article, however much they may look like it. On the other hand there have been introductions of the genuine polecat to parts of the Highlands in recent years: all privately arranged and not talked about. So, despite what I've said in the opening lines, you may well be lucky enough to meet the real thing.

In the true polecat the outer coat is long and dark with a purplish sheen, and this parts readily to reveal the buff under-fur. There is a mask of dark fur enclosing the eyes and extending over the muzzle. This is framed in white or near-white, giving the impression that the animal is wearing spectacles.

Dog polecats weigh up to two and three-quarter pounds, and measure almost two feet in overall length. Bitches are smaller.

AMERICAN MINK

Nowadays you are liable to meet up with the mink in almost any part of Scotland. These animals are the descendants of escapes from fur farms. They have proved viable, and breed well, and have taken the place once occupied by the polecat. Wild mink come in a variety of colours, but the best survivors are of the ancestral type. This is rich, dark brown in colour, almost black, with a white spot on the lower lip. Most trapped animals are like this, and trapped animals are the ones people most often use. On average, the mink is about the size of a polecat-ferret.

GREY OR ATLANTIC SEAL

Once the grey seals come ashore to breed, the red deer takes second place as Scotland's largest land animal. A bull grey seal is more than three times the weight of a good Highland stag.

This seal is land-based during the entire breeding season, and

The common seal is numerous in shallow waters

as all its important breeding stations are known, it isn't difficult to meet up with once you've solved the problem of getting to them. The main stations are on North Rona, the Inner and Outer Hebrides, Orkney and Shetland. There are small colonies, numbered in hundreds compared with the thousands on the islands, along the north and east coasts.

At some stations the seals will cover the entire island; on North Rona they move up to 250 feet above sea level; elsewhere the pups are born on beaches and skerries, in sheltered coves, and sometimes in sea caves.

There is no harem system. Where the red stags hold hinds rather than ground, the bull seals hold ground rather than cows. The cows come and go as they please, and are mated by the bull on whose territory they happen to be when ready. Mating may therefore be by one bull several times, or by several bulls in succession.

Delayed implantation lasts until mid-Feburary into March. Single pups are the rule. At birth the pup will weigh from twenty to forty-two pounds, and puts on about four pounds a day. At the age of three weeks, when it is deserted by the cow, it will weigh over one hundred pounds. Once it has been deserted it wanders about the station, losing weight at the rate of one pound a day, until it is ready to go to sea and fend for itself.

The cow seal defends the area round her pup; the bull his whole stamping ground. If harassed, or too much disturbed, the cows will desert their pups, and sometimes you'll find a cow nursing a pup that is not her own. After mating the cows return to the sea, and begin feeding after their three weeks' fast. The bulls may fast for the whole two months of the season, but it is unlikely that many bulls can last right through it in possession of their territory.

COMMON SEAL

The common seal is most numerous in shallow waters on sandy and muddy coasts, round most of Scotland, and out to the

Northern and Western Isles. It is abundant on the Moray Firth and in the Tay estuary.

Harbour seal is another name for this species. The usual colour is dark grey above and lighter grey on the underside, with darker leopard spotting all over. There are light and dark phases but the leopard spotting is always apparent. Pups are like the adults, except for a few that are born white. These change to grey in a day or two. Both sexes can be distinguished from the grey seal at all times by their snub noses and slanted nostrils.

Unlike the grey seal this species doesn't come ashore to breed. The pups are born either in the water, or on a rock from which they float away on the first tide. From the start they are active and able to swim, unlike the grey seal pups which are helpless. The common seal cow is very attentive to her pup, rolling and playing with it in the water, and flippering it to safety in rough seas or through heavy swells.

Having no close season and no statutory protection, common seals can be killed at any time; but there has never been the public outcry against this that there has been over the controversial grey seal cull. Man is its most important predator, killing it for its pelt or when he considers it an important competitor for flatfish. The killer whale has been recorded as a sometimes predator.

HARES

There are two species of hare in Scotland: the brown hare, and the blue or mountain hare. It would be an over-simplification to suggest that the brown hare is the one of the Lowlands, and the blue that of the Highlands, although it is largely true. But the blue hares often come down, in certain areas, to ground occupied by the brown, and in recent years the brown has been colonising into the glens on to ground properly that of the blue. So the twain do meet, and therefore confuse the unwary observer.

The blue hare is smaller and more thick-set than the brown,

with a bigger head, shorter legs and shorter ears: but none of these characteristics is obvious in the field. Tail colour is the diagnostic feature; it is white above and below. The brown hare's tail is black above and white below. The blue hare in winter coat can be confused with nothing else, for then it moults to white. Apart from the stoat it is the only Scottish mammal to do so.

Mountains and high moorland are the terrain of this hare: from 1,000 to 2,500 feet, although it will range to the highest tops. During storms and blizzards, or prolonged snow, the hares move to lower ground, and can be seen in forests and scrub. At the 1,000 to 1,500 feet contour the ranges of the blue and the brown hare overlap.

March is the peak mating season, but typical rowdy assemblies can be seen in February when snow is covering the ground. Like the brown hare the blues box, and leap, and chase each other, leaving moulted fur snagged on heather all over the area. After mating, the doe moves away on its own. When her young are due she scrapes a form for them in the heather, or she may have them in a peat shelter, or even in a burrow. Unlike brown hares the blues use burrows and shelters regularly, and will dig through snow to get to them.

The leverets are born furred, and with their eyes open, and are active from the first day of life. Like the adults, they are preyed upon by eagles, foxes and wildcats. Buzzards and stoats take leverets of a size they can handle.

Blue hares feed at dusk and through the night, but when snow is lying they do so at all hours. Like the brown hare and the rabbit the blue hare reswallows its soft daytime droppings, which are then passed through the digestive system a second time. This is known as reingestion or refection. The hard purlies with which everyone is familiar are the seconds.

The brown hare is big-toothed, and big-whiskered, with long hindlegs and long, black-tipped ears. It will reach two feet in length, exclusive of tail, and weigh from seven to nine pounds or more. This hare likes open, undulating country, up to 1,500 feet and down to sea level. It is notable for its riotous March assemblies; outside this period it is a solitary animal.

Speed and endurance, and a high degree of courage and cunning, are the brown hare's defences in the fight for survival. It is built for speed and is at its best uphill, which is the way it will run if it can. When turned, it will run a diagonal rather than a straight descent, for the long hindlegs put it at a disadvantage on a fast downhill chase. Depending on its size and condition this hare is preyed upon by foxes, eagles, wildcats, ravens, buzzards, dogs, stoats and even weasels. But man is the main predator.

Leverets have been found in every month of the year, but most are born between February and August. They can run about soon after birth. Not all young conceived are born. Some embryos die in the womb and are resorbed into the mother's tissues (resorption). In other cases the hare can become pregnant while pregnant (superfoetation). The latter isn't a new discovery. Pliny knew about it and wrote about it a long time ago.

RABBIT

The rabbit is found all over Scotland, from the machairs of the isles to the glens, farmlands, woodlands, hedgerows, sand dunes, salt marshes and moorlands of the mainland. Since myxomatosis the population in many of these habitats is skeletal. In general, rabbits are less numerous than they were before the disease struck; locally, numbers rise and fall as it comes and goes.

Unlike the hares, rabbits are social animals, living in burrow systems called warrens. In each colony there is a hierarchical system or peck order. Mature males, usually heavyweights, dominate all other bucks in the colony; lesser bucks always give way to them. Dominant does behave similarly towards lesser females, including young. Very young males are often bullied into leaving the colony by master bucks. Displaced young either hive off into new colonies or return to the warren later in the year when it is safe to do so.

The doe rabbit makes her nest of grass or hay, mixed with wool plucked from her body. The most secure nests are those in the main warren. Away from it such nests are more vulnerable, for they are in short tunnels, from one to three feet deep. The doe pads earth over the entrance between visits, but in time this becomes mixed with wool from her feet, and the site becomes obvious. Young rabbits are born blind and naked. They are weaned at three weeeks and are on their own when a month old.

Predators that kill hares also kill rabbits. Very small weaners are killed by owls and kestrels, and even weasels.

SQUIRRELS

There are two species of squirrel in Scotland: the native red and the alien American grey. The relationship between them is obscure. The grey has taken over ground not much favoured by the red, but also ground once held in strength by it. Such a

The grey squirrel is a major pest

39

takeover implies competition of some kind, but the method isn't known, and is probably complex and subtle. One certainty seems to be that the red cannot retake ground once it is held by greys. When both occupy the same habitat for a time it is a mere changing of the guard: from red to grey.

The red squirrel's strongholds are the dark coniferous forests, and it is still common in such places. Nowadays it is practically unknown in the central lowlands, which are now the grey's strongholds. The grey hasn't yet reached the Highland line, but it will soon be knocking against it.

Squirrel nests are called dreys. The red squirrel's drey, built with twigs and lined with moss, leaves and bits of bark, is usually built more than twenty feet from the ground. It has no obvious entrance or exit; the squirrel has to force an entry at each visit. The average litter is three, but litters up to six have been recorded. The young at birth are blind and toothless, with whiskers but no hair. At the age of two months they are independent and active in the vicinity of the nest.

In broad-leaved woodland red squirrels spend some time on the ground, scraping in the leaf litter, often when burying or uncovering food. In coniferous woodland, or forest, they seem to spend little time on the ground. They are true tree squirrels, and when surprised on the ground they have one escape route: up, into a tree: or something. Barrett-Hamilton recorded the story of a red squirrel, confronted by a Highlander and his dog on a treeless moor, climbing the man to escape from the dog. Getting a tree between itself and an intruder is a habit of the red squirrel, and when the intruder is a man it will go up and round the trunk, keeping the man in sight while itself remaining hidden.

Squirrels don't hibernate. During the wild weather they will lie up for a time; but they are active throughout the winter on fine or fair days. They store surplus food, usually by burying it, but sometimes by hiding it in holes in trees. Some animals store a lot of food in one cache; more often the squirrels bury it all over the place, and maybe forget about most of it. Big stores of hazel nuts or acorns, attributed to squirrels, are more often than not the work of fieldmice.

The grey squirrel is a major pest, and provides a good

example of the danger of introducing alien species. This one was actively encouraged by man to settle, and now everybody regrets it. About thirty attempts were made by various people to get it to settle. One expatriate American turned over a hundred of them loose from a private collection. It is now an offence to turn grey squirrels loose, or to keep them in captivity without a licence.

This American is a hustler and a thruster, strong and knowing how to use its strength. An adult is a handful for anything smaller than itself, including predators. It has been recorded killing stoat and rat. A grey squirrel at a bird table in winter is in complete control until it chooses to leave. I have watched one chasing Leghorn pullets from their grain and another driving away a fiery Ancona cockerel in squawking flight.

Mixed deciduous woodland, including oak and beech, is the grey squirrel's preferred habitat. It builds its drey in the fork of a tree. The oak is a favourite nesting place, and of course it provides food as well: acorns, young leaves, buds and shoots. The female will raise six or seven young in a season. She takes great care of them, and will defend them even against a marauding cat. Mortality among young in the nest appears to be low, and if they survive past adolescence they have a reasonable chance of living for four or five years.

VOLES

Voles, like mice and rats, are rodents. And to most people voles are mice of a sort. Indeed, when the woodmouse was known as the fieldmouse, the field vole was known as the short-tailed fieldmouse, although they belong to different families. There should really be no confusion. Mice and rats are long-tailed and long-faced, with prominent ears, whereas voles are short-tailed, blunt-faced, small-eared and beady-eyed.

The biggest of the family is the water vole, which is rat size, with tail more than half the body length. The fur is rich dark brown above, paler and sometimes greyer on the underside. In 41 the Highlands most water voles are black. Like other voles the water vole is short-lived. Few survive their second winter, although captive animals will live much longer.

Unfortunately for the water vole it is frequently mistaken for the brown rat, and harried accordingly. The mistake is easy enough to understand, for brown rats frequently live afield in the summer months, and often enough take over the burrows of water voles. Rats will kill young voles, as invading weasels do.

Water voles hold linear territories, upstream and down, for a hundred yards or more, and this stretch the master defends fiercely. There will be many burrows along it, but only the master's mate and offspring will be using them. Upstream and down are latrines, scented from the vole's flank glands, and with droppings clearly displayed where no prospecting vole could miss them. Such are the vole's territory markers.

Males probably hold their territory for life, while females are more unsettled. Breeding starts in March and lasts into September or October. Litter size varies with the age and size of the mother, but four or five young are usual, and there will be four litters or more in a season. Early litters stand a better chance of surviving the winter than later ones, and these form the next year's breeding stock.

Breeding nests are usually underground, but in wet places they may be under a tree root or among rushes. In bank sites the female plugs the entrance to her nursery with grass and mud, and the grass is usually grazed around them. Close grazing around burrow entrances is typical. The main foods are the grasses and reeds that grow by the waterside, but the vole will eat a wide variety of vegetable food, including beech mast and stubble grain. Infrequently it will turn carnivore and eat sparingly of water snails or freshwater mussels.

The field vole is brown above and grey below, with a tail less than half its body length. It is blunt-faced and short-legged, with ears almost hidden in the fur. Size varies from under five inches to over six inches in length, including tail. Weight varies not only with the season, but with the density of voles on the ground. Spring weights are heaviest; then a big male will go to well over an ounce.

The bank vole is active and agile

Field voles prefer rough grassland; grass is their food and their cover. Young plantations make ideal habitats, and fair numbers are found on sheep walks. But they are found on all marginal grassland, and on heather moorland, even to the Alpine plateaux of the Cairngorms. They are thinly distributed in scrub and woodland, but will invade hayfields, especially in areas where the hay ripens late.

This vole is notable for its population ups and downs, or cycles. In mixed woodland or mixed scrubland there are no such cycles. But in monocultures of young trees or grassland they have conditions that are ideal: in both there is grass in abundance. In both there is little or no diversification of plant species. Such monocultures, or near monocultures, are defined by the ecologist as simple habitats: and in such simple habitats the voles increase and decrease on a four or five year cycle, often spectacularly.

The number of voles on an acre of ground can be as few as five to ten, or as many as 600 or more at the peak of a cycle. The peak is followed by a spectacular crash in numbers; then there is a period of low density; then the cycle begins all over again. On such ground the predators increase as the voles increase, and go down as the voles go down. They are related to the cycle, and adjust to it; but they cannot control it. They can't even keep pace with it. In winter, however, when the voles are not breeding, and when their cover is poor, a strong predator force can reduce numbers significantly.

The breeding season extends from March to October, sometimes even later, and occasionally goes on right through the winter. The first young of the year are independent by May. Young voles can, and do, breed from the age of three weeks, but this depends on the state of the population cycle. In a peak year, the young animals stay small, or grow slowly, and may not breed at all. When numbers are low they breed early. Voles come on heat every three or four days, even when suckling, so that a mother can become pregnant while nursing a family.

On ground well stocked with voles their signs are everywhere. The rough grass is honeycombed with the entrances to their surface runs, or creeps. Trackways are everywhere. Voles are often sighted. Under tufts of grass there will be little platforms of chopped grass. These platforms are often used as latrines; more usually the droppings are scattered along the trackways.

The field vole is the bread and butter of the hunters. Every predator, bird or mammal, specialist or opportunist, will eat it. The short-eared owl is a specialist, and settles in areas with plenty of voles. In the Carron Valley, Stirlingshire, the owls held forty-five acres of territory during a vole plague; after it was over most of them moved out, and those remaining extended their territories to 400 acres.

The bank vole, although blunt-faced, is more mouse-like in profile than the field vole, and redder in colour. The ears are partly hidden in the fur, and the tail is at least half the length of the body. Although less robustly built, the bank vole reaches about the same overall length and weight. Young animals born late overwinter at a small size, then grow in the spring.

This species prefers deciduous woodland, and scrub with plenty of ground cover. It also likes hedgerows and banks where brambles and other trailing or creeping plants grow thickly. It has been recorded at 2,500 feet.

The female bank vole builds her breeding nest of grass, moss and bark, all finely shredded, and it may be above ground or below. Nests above ground are built in thick cover or in a mossy stump. The breeding season is from April to October, during which the female will have four or five litters. Spring litters will be about four young; summer litters may be five; later litters about three. The female can become pregnant while suckling.

Besides the leaves and stems of plants, berries, seeds, fungi and roots, bank voles eat insects and their larvae. They have been recorded eating field vole. They take fewer insects than woodmice do; otherwise their food is about the same.

This vole is active and agile, a scurrier and a climber, a hunter of thick cover that makes forays into the open then darts back into hiding again. It does not use grass tunnels, or creeps, like the field vole. It burrows just beneath the surface, and digs deeper shafts, often under tree roots, to its sleeping quarters. The weasel is the only hunter that can invade these burrows, but they are frequently used by other voles, and sometimes shrews.

Bank voles appear on the prey list of most bird and mammal predators, but not as often as one might think, considering their numbers.

The Orkney vole is confined to Orkney, where it occurs on all the bigger islands except Hoy and Shapinsay. It is closely related to the continental vole, and is similar to the field vole of the mainland, except that it is larger and darker. It is found on farmlands and rough grazings up to the 700 feet contour.

MICE AND RATS

The house mouse isn't found in as many houses as it used to be: like the human flea it is becoming scarcer in such places. Yet, wherever man is the mouse will try to be. In its place of origin in the Far East it can still be found living on dry steppe and feeding on grass. When it associates with man, as in this country, its feeding habits change. While it can live afield indefinitely it takes the first opportunity to get back with man. The late Sir Frank Fraser Darling has told how, when he was living on Lunga of the Treshnish Isles, the house mice moved into his camp, although they had been living wild for eighty years.

Ever since its arrival in this country the house mouse has lived largely at man's expense: eating his food, fouling his food, occupying his buildings, gnawing at his clothing, and leaving an unpleasant smell. In the days before the combine harvester, when grain was stacked in farmyards, it swarmed in the stacks, making meal of the ickers, and fouling them with its droppings. In the corn stacks the mice could double their numbers every two months, and there could be as many as fifteen of them to a cubic yard. The local weasels and barn owls took their toll, but could make no impression on their numbers.

Yet there has always been an element of whimsy in people's attitude to the house mouse. It has figured prominently in poem, story, cartoon strip and cinema. Disney made it immortal. Even in more serious affairs it crept in, as when England enacted against Sinn Fein hunger strikers released from Mountjoy jail, and the Irish called the legislation The Cat and Mouse Act.

In good habitats (for example the old stackyards) the house mouse could produce up to ten litters a year. In less favoured habitats it produced five or six litters.

The woodmouse is the handsome, sprightly fieldmouse that Burns wrote about. The wife of a stalker friend of mine called it "the nice moose" as distinct from the house mouse which she called "the ordinary moose". She knew the difference.

Woodmice are quite like house mice, but more reddish, with longer hindlegs, bigger ears, much larger eyes, a more massive snout and a very long tail. Sometimes there is a patch of orange on the throat; sometimes there isn't. The young, being greyer, are more likely to be confused with house mice.

In woodland and scrub, and in the hedgerows of cultivated fields, woodmice are most at home. But they are hardy animals, and will be found in small numbers in open fields and hill country, in ruined crofts and old drystane dykes. They range

Woodmice are most at home in woodland and scrub

widely over the treeless Hebridean islands. They are found in gardens and orchards, but only rarely enter houses, although this appears to be happening more frequently in country places.

The woodmouse's breeding nest, built of chopped and shredded grass, may be below ground or under a heap of branches or hedge clippings. When underground it is at the end of a short burrow. Permanent nests can be as deep as three feet. Because of this the woodmouse is a difficult animal to dig out, and many a fox has scraped over a big area of woodland in the attempt. Weasels are something else; they can go down the burrows and catch the mouse at home. Other predators are the stoat, the tawny owl and long-eared owl. Foxes, when not wasting time digging for adults, kill a lot of young. Farm cats take their share.

Man and woodmouse sometimes clash, because it can do a lot of damage in a garden, eating crocus, lily and hyacinth bulbs, and peas. It has been reported entering a beehive and eating comb, and it certainly eats bumble bee grubs. Its range of food is wide: fruit, nuts, seeds, green plants, fungi, snails, spiders, adult

47

insects and their larvae, and occasionally the eggs and young of small birds. The proportion of these foods taken depends on locality, season, and the age and sex of the mice.

Woodmice store food, usually underground but sometimes in the old nests of hedgerow birds. Sometimes such a nest is roofed over by the mouse and used as a shelter as well as a store. There is a record of such a store in a rook's nest. I've found both mouse and food store in the hollowed-out bike of the common wasp. Being good climbers the mice can harvest hips, haws and rowans in trees and hedges. They open hazel nuts by nibbling a hole to extract the kernel; in the same way they gnaw a hole in the shells of snails.

Although they squeak, they are not usually noisy. Nor are they aggressively territorial. Individuals and family groups have home ranges, but there is much coming and going across the frontiers and a lot of mixing. The young remain on good terms with their parents until long after maturity.

The harvest mouse is the smallest mouse but not the smallest mammal. It is reddish brown above and white below, with a clear demarcation line between the zones. It is a slim, delicate mouse, blunt-nosed and beady-eyed, with short, rounded ears and a prehensile tail that is used as a fifth hand.

This mouse was once reported on the east coast as far north as Aberdeen. It is persistently reported from the Border counties. Recently it has been certainly recorded as far north as Edinburgh. But what its status is in Scotland nobody really knows.

The globe breeding nest of this species is well known from photographs and drawings, but not many people have seen the real thing. The nest is woven from stems, grass blades, and other vegetation, secured to several corn stalks or reeds or other strong growth, and placed up to one foot from the ground. It is lined with shredded grass and soft roots. It is opened by the mouse when she is leaving or entering, and closed when she is inside.

The brown rat, like the house mouse an alien species, is well known to everybody, and survives in a variety of habitats: in town and country, from mountain to seashore. It is the most serious and costly mammal pest in our history.

Not so long ago I wrote that the brown rat was tough, resourceful, cunning and aggressive; wasteful and provident; clean and dirty; hidebound yet highly adaptable; quick to learn and slow to forget. That is still how I would sum it up.

A big rat will face man, dog, cat or weasel when cornered; it will do it even when not cornered, if it thinks its escape route is cut off. A female defending young will put a kitten to flight, maul a kit weasel, make hole in a terrier's face, or bite a man. Rat bites, rat fleas, and rat urine are all potential disease hazards to man.

A fully grown rat will measure from fourteen to nineteen inches, including tail of six and a half to nine inches. Weight varies with sex and age but typical adults will weigh about a pound. My terrier killed one weighing a pound and three-quarters.

In good habitats, with plenty of food and cover, rats will breed right through the year, but only for part of the year when living the harder life afield. Even when there is breeding throughout the year the females do not all breed at the same time, or all the time. They will have from three to five litters, numbering from two to fourteen, and many of them will be pregnant while suckling.

Although wasteful and destructive, the rat is a food hoarder in its own interest. I've watched five rats ferrying away and caching a pound of whole oats. When I put down hen eggs, weighing two and a quarter ounces each, the rats rolled them away, using nose and chin, and heaved them over obstacles with their forepaws. One killed a number of fortnight-old pullets by tearing them on the throat and neck.

Having its regular runways, and being familiar with every yard of them, a rat will pull up short at any strange object in its path. Once it loses its fear of the object the rat will go over or round it. If it goes round it the loop becomes part of the runway, and it will continue to use the loop for twenty-four hours or more after the object has been removed.

The black rat, which reached Britain probably in the eleventh century, has been replaced over most of the UK by the brown rat, and its status in Scotland is not known. It probably still exists in Orkney and the Shiants, and may turn up in unexpected places through being accidentally transported by man.

HEDGEHOG

The hedgehog, the biggest of our so-called insectivorous mammals, is probably the one that nobody ever mistakes for anything else. On its upper side it is protected, from crown to root of tail by an armour of dark brown quills; the underside is coarse-furred like the head and tail. The hedgehog's defence posture is to coil into a ball, thus presenting an enemy with an unbroken array of bristling thorns. In newly born young the spines are sparse and pliable; they harden and darken by the age of four weeks, and thereafter become denser.

Just how well the hedgehog is protected by its quilled armour depends on the will and weaponry of the attacker. The badger

The hedgehog is well protected by quilled armour

can tear one open without much trouble; a persistent fox, with enough time and hunger, can do it. The Staffordshire bull terrier is reputed to be an expert at it, which certainly isn't true of dogs in general. Very young hedgehogs are more vulnerable, and the tawny owl has been recorded as a predator. But man and the motor vehicle are probably the greatest killers of all.

Young hedgehogs have been recorded in every month from May to October. The peak littering months are May and June, and many animals breed twice in the year. Common nesting sites are rabbit burrows, tree roots and hedgebottoms. The male takes no part in rearing the family. The female will move her family to a new nest if disturbed, and may desert them if the disturbance continues.

The prey range is wide: beetles, earthworms, slugs, snails, caterpillars, pupae and woodlice, and anything else the beast can catch and hold: mice, voles, lizards, frogs, small rabbits and rats. It will take the eggs and nestlings of small birds, but these form only a small part of its food. Being an opportunist, it will eat pig meal, poultry pellets, kipper skins, and the scrapings of the camper's frying pan. Hedgehogs kill adders; just how often is anybody's guess. But they are not immune to the snake's venom. I knew two hedgehogs that died after being struck on the nose. The snakes, bleeding about the mouth, lived.

Male hedgehogs fight with each other in spring, which indicates territorial dispute. When the young are out of the nest, male and female can be seen together with them.

Hedgehogs hibernate, making a warm winter nest under the roots of a tree, in a banking or in deep leaf litter. An animal well fatted up in autumn will go through without a break, and I know one that slept for 127 days after I found it. A hedgehog on foot in winter is not likely to survive.

MOLE

The mole is found in every Scottish county, and is most numerous on good arable land and in deciduous woodland. It will also be found on good hill pastures, up to 1,500 feet. It avoids peaty moorland and coniferous forest.

Most of the mole's life is spent underground eating, burrowing and sleeping – and it is wonderfully adapted for its lifestyle. It has enormous, strongly muscled, spade-like forefeet, a pointed face, a cylindrical body with no obvious neck, no external ears, and small eyes deeply hidden by erect fur that can't be "rubbed the wrong way". The fur is slate grey to black, fine, short, and dense.

Moleheaps are a familiar sight; moles alive on the surface are not. But they do surface from time to time, especially in spring and summer, or during a drought. The beast will show its face when putting up its heaps, or when it is working just under the surface, as it often does in loose, rich soil. A lot of moleheaps doesn't mean a lot of moles. Very big heaps, of the order of a barrow load of soil, are the so-called fortresses, in which there will be a sleeping nest with bolt runs into the main tunnels, or even a breeding nest with young. Breeding nests are more usually underground, with nothing overhead to betray them.

The mole's life is spent underground

The speed at which a mole tunnels depends on the nature of the soil and the amount of prey it is finding. In a rich seam it drives slowly. The beast hunts as it tunnels, then uses the tunnels for moving about in, so they are also a communication system. Most of them are less than a foot deep; others go much deeper. Voles and shrews use the tunnels at times, and a weasel will travel through them to get across a field without showing itself.

Earthworms, millipedes, snails and caterpillars make up the bulk of the mole's food. Earthworms are the most important, and the mole will disable and store a surplus. In turn, it is preyed on by foxes, badgers, stoats, weasels, herons, owls, buzzards and kestrels. Young moles, on the move after independence, are the commonest victims. Man is the most important predator on moles of all ages at all times.

SHREWS

The common shrew has pinhead eyes, long whiskers, and a flexible, trunk-like snout. Fully grown it weighs less than half an ounce. It is a hunter of the undergrowth and the ground litter, and is found from sea level to mountain tops.

Where shrews squeak (and they squeak a lot) they can, with patience, be seen by parting the cover, although at first the only sign may be the heaving of the ground litter. But sooner or later the shrew will break out, questing with its snout, pouncing on a woodlouse here, a spider there, or an earthworm uncovered by the upheaval. They make less noise in winter and are therefore more difficult to find, but they are still working round the clock, and active under the deepest snow.

The appetite of the shrew is prodigious, and it has to eat more than its own body weight in twenty-four hours. It dies if deprived of food for more than a few hours. So it has to live at high pressure, sleeping between bouts of eating. It is always vocal, always quarrelsome, and frequently aggressive towards other shrews. Shrew fights shrew, but fights are rarely mortal. When

53

one shrew kills another it will be a male fighting another male over a female in season.

In April most females are pregnant. Litter size varies from one to ten; the number of litters from one to three in the season. Breeding stops between August and October, by which time most of the old animals have died off. Few shrews live to see their second autumn.

Mammalian predators kill shrews but don't often eat them, unless the alternatives are shrew or famine. Bird predators, on the other hand, eat them readily. Owls and kestrels carry them to the nest when feeding chicks.

The pygmy shrew weighs less than a quarter of an ounce; otherwise it closely resembles the common shrew. It is not the most common but it is the most widely distributed species, being found all over the mainland and on most of the islands. It isn't found on St Kilda, Shetland or North Rona.

It occupies the same kind of ground as the common shrew, hunts the same kind of food, and requires up to double its own body weight every day. It has a similar life-span. It vies with the pipistrelle bat for the title of Scotland's smallest mammal.

The water shrew is the biggest and heaviest of the clan, weighing up to about half an ounce, depending on sex and age. It is usually, but not always, a black and white shrew, black above and white below, with a clear line of demarcation along the flanks. But the black sometimes has a flush of dark brown, and the under-fur may be greyish white or cream. The tail is dark brown on top, and whitish on the underside where there is an obvious keel, or fin, of swimming hairs.

Clear, unpolluted pools and streams are the habitat of this shrew, but it will live and breed in woodland or on moorland some distance from the nearest water. I've seen it brought to the nest of tawny owls in tall woodland a mile from the nearest stream. Waterside shrews eat insects, crustaceans, snails, small fishes and frogs. Away from water they probably hunt the same prey as the other two shrews.

The water shrew is an accomplished swimmer and diver. It can enter the water as quietly as an otter, but when it dives from a bank it makes a distinct *plop*. It swims high, wiggling like a

The common shrew has a prodigious appetite

tadpole, dog-paddling with its forefeet. Underwater it uses its hair-finned tail as a rudder; the bristles on its forefeet act like webs. Air bubbles trapped in the fur often give it a silvery appearance when swimming underwater. Like the dipper it can hunt the bottom, turning over pebbles in search of prey.

The breeding season is from May to September, and two litters of five or six are usual, the females becoming pregnant soon after the birth of the first. Nests are usually in the bank not far from the water. They are loosely built of grass and withered leaves, with upper and lower exits in the bank.

On land the water shrew is faster than the others, and runs with ferret-like bounds. There it literally swims though the litter, hunting woodlice, earthworms and spiders. It hunts round the clock and the year.

BATS

Bats are the only flying mammals. In Scotland they used to be called bauckie birds. The bauckies of Scotland come in four species, more or less common: pipistrelle, Daubenton's bat, long-eared bat and natterer's bat. Bats find their way, and their prey, by echo-location; by uttering short-wave squeaks that are reflected back by any object in their path.

Pipistrelle is found all over Scotland, and on most of the off-shore islands. It is common in towns and villages as well as in the countryside. Although it haunts buildings, it occurs where there is none, and is found in trees and rock clefts whether near human habitations or not. This is the smallest bat, with a wingspan of under eight inches and weighing not more than one-fifth of an ounce.

Bat-light for pipistrelle in summer is sunset, and it will be hawking before the owls are on the wing. It takes most, if not all, of its prey on the wing. Many types of insect are taken but gnats appear to be the main prey. Most prey is eaten on the wing, but larger ones are carried to some favourite eating place to be dealt with there.

Mating takes place in autumn and winter, the female storing the male sperms in her body and becoming fertilised in the spring. The single young is born in the second half of June, or the first half of July. The flying season is from March to October, but pipistrelle will appear in any month in sunny weather. I watched three on a February day at Loch Tulla, when Rannoch was blanketed with snow and the drifts were three feet deep. They were wavering among the pines and breasting the snowdrifts, as talkative as on a summer evening.

The long-eared bat is bigger than pipistrelle, with a wingspan of about ten inches. It is a common species, easily recognisable, even in flight, because of its extraordinarily long ears, which are almost as long as the head and body together. In summer it sleeps in buildings and trees; it hibernates in caves or buildings, sometimes in trees.

This bat comes out after sunset and hunts on and off during the night. Prey is caught mostly on the foliage and trunks of trees, but some is caught in flight. The flight is moth-like, with occasional glides, and the bat hunts from hedge height to tree height, hovering among the foliage like a bee at a foxglove bell.

It is also agile on roofs and walls. During its spells of hunting the long-ear alights frequently to dismember prey, and the strippings from beetles and other insects can be seen at such places.

Mating takes place in October/November or in April/May, the first being of mature animals and the second of animals too young to breed in the autumn. A single young is born in June or July.

Daubenton's bat is found in Scotland as far north as Elgin, and there are isolated records north of there. This is the water bat, hunting all its prey over water, and is the one usually caught on the fisherman's fly. But it can be confused with pipistrelle which hunts over water some of the time. It has a wingspan of up to ten inches.

This bat is a deceptively fast flyer. On summer nights a number of them can be seen hunting together, hawking low over the water like swallows, and breaking the surface to drink on the wing. Mist will send them higher, and a drop in temperature, with frost, will send them to roost, perhaps for the rest of the night. Usually they will hunt on and off during the night until

Natterer's bat has a wingspan of ten to eleven inches

just before sunrise, and are not put off by light rain. The food is almost entirely aquatic insects, taken on the wing, and includes dragonflies and large moths.

During the summer months Daubenton's bat roosts in holes in trees or rocks, as well as in caves and buildings. If you slap the trunk of a tree where these bats are roosting, just before they are due to come out, they will leave the hole squeaking and sizzling in protest. A single young is born in June or July.

Natterer's bat is recorded from time to time in a few areas in the south of Scotland. It has a wingspan from ten to eleven inches. It frequents woodland and timbered parkland, often near water. The food consists of insects and spiders. A single young is born in late June or early July.

REPTILES AND AMPHIBIANS

SNAKE AND LIZARDS

SCOTLAND has one snake and two lizards; no more. The snake is the adder. Any grass snake you find will be somebody's escaped pet, or an escape from a private collection. One of the lizards looks like a snake, but isn't: it is the legless slow-worm. The other is the common or viviparous lizard.

The adder is venomous. It's so-called bite is really a strike. In this country adder-bite isn't usually a matter of life or death. Fatalities are rare; perhaps one in half a century. By and large, adders are in more danger from people than people are from adders.

A fully grown female adder in Scotland will reach two feet in length, or a little more: males are smaller, almost always under two feet. Adders of two and a half feet or more are pipe dreams or escaped grass snakes. The snake has a small head, a narrow neck, and a thick muscular body, tapering quickly at the tail. It has the V-sign behind the head and a dark zig-zag line along the spine. In females the markings may be faint, but they can still be seen; in the more contrasty males they are obvious.

Young adders are born in autumn, usually August, escaping from the rupturing egg sacs at the moment of extrusion. They are about the length of a pencil, and venomous from birth, although to begin with they feed on small prey: insects and the like. Young and adults go into hibernation in October, emerging in spring. Group hibernation is not unusual. The pairing season is in May.

The forked tongue is a sense organ; it gathers scent impressions which are then transmitted to the brain. When the snake strikes a prey – lizard, mouse or vole – the animal does not die at once. It usually escapes into cover to die there. The adder, using its tongue, tracks it by scent.

The harmless slow-worm should never be mistaken for an adder. It is a lizard without legs. Its skin is smooth and sheened. Colour varies: bronze, brass, chestnut, brown, grey and near-gold. Like other lizards it can blink its eyes, which adders can't do. It gives birth to living young, most of the eggs rupturing beforehand. At birth the young are three to four inches long, and have black flanks and belly. They are born in August or September.

Slow-worms prey on a variety of slugs, earthworms, insects and their larvae. The small white slug *Agrolemix agrestis* is a common item. Many species prey on slow-worms: adders, foxes, buzzards, eagles, badgers, hedgehogs, crows and ravens. Any hunter of big earthworms is likely to take young slow-worms, because they are about the right size and move in much the same way.

The common or viviparous lizard looks what it is: a lizard. It is small; not more than five and a half inches including its very long, tapering tail. Males have brilliant orange or vermilion bellies, heavily spotted with black; the bellies of females are pale orange, yellow, blue or grey, with few black spots or none at all.

The breeding season is in April and May, and the young are born free of the egg sac in July, August or September. Apart from their small size (less than two inches) they are bronze or black in colour, so are easily distinguished from adults. They almost double this size before going into hibernation in October.

Prey is mostly spiders, flies, larvae, grasshoppers, and other small invertebrates. Earthworms, although sometimes taken, are not a common item. The lizard swallows small prey whole; bigger prey it shakes like a terrier shaking a rat. It is preyed upon in turn by adders, foxes, crows, buzzards and the like, but

The common frog isn't as common as it used to be

it isn't an easy catch for any of them.

Under stress, or when carelessly handled, it will part with its tail, which is specially designed for this kind of self fracture, known as autotony, and under the control of the lizard. As a protective mechanism it often works, the front end of the lizard escaping while the predator is left with the tail. The lizard grows a new tail, which is made of gristle instead of bone.

FROGS, TOAD AND NEWTS

The common frog isn't as common as it used to be; nor has it the number of variety of spawning places – ponds, ditches, pools – it used to have. But it is still common enough, confused only with the toad, although it shouldn't be. The frog is the high-jumping, long-jumping, volatile activist; with smooth, sheened skin and peaked back. It comes in many colour phases. Red frogs are well known in the northwest and the west. Yellow types, with black leopard markings, and near-blacks, occur in the far north. 61

Males are smaller and less robust than females, and always have a pad on the first fingers.

Frogs spawn from low ground up to 1,500 feet, even in places liable to near drying out. I knew one such place on Atholl where the tadpoles survived when the puddle became ooze. They grew very slowly, and overwintered as tadpoles. At spawning time the frogs are vocal. Modern evidence suggests that they find their way to their own ponds by scent. The tadpoles become tiny frogs by late summer, when they leave the water, as agile as fleas.

Hibernation begins in October, usually in or near water, but sometimes away from it. Many frogs bury themselves in the mud at the bottom of ponds and ditches. In such places they get enough oxygen through the skin to keep them alive. But if ice covers the pond for too long in spring, sealing the frogs in, skin oxygen isn't enough and the animals may drown before reaching air. Many frogs die at this time for a variety of reasons. The predator force of herons, hedgehogs, ducks, ravens, crows, buzzards, eagles, mink, pine martens, stoats, weasels, rats, wildcats and foxes takes its toll.

The toad is the warty, squat crawler with the topaz eyes. Most are dark in colour, with grey or olive overtones. A clean toad in full bloom looks as though clad in leopard skin.

Frogs and toads are regularly found in the same ponds or pools, but usually spawn in different parts of them. Toad spawn is a black-dotted clear ribbon trailed round water plants, unlike the polka-dotted jelly mass laid by the frog. The toads leave the water soon after spawning, and disperse into the countryside. They are much more land animals than frogs. They hibernate on land, from October or November until early spring, and return to the same pond year after year. The warts have a toxic secretion which is some sort of defence against predators, but many predators attack toads and some of them eat them.

Scotland has all three British newts, but their distribution is different. The palmate newt is the one found over most of the mainland. The smooth newt and the warty newt are widely distributed, but are absent from whole areas, especially in the north and northeast.

READING LIST

Darling, F Fraser and J Morton, *The Highlands and Islands*, Collins, 1969

Darling, F Fraser, *A Herd of Red Deer*, Oxford University Press, 1937

Godfrey, G K and P Crowcroft, *The Life of the Mole*, Museum Press, 1960

Hewer, H R, *British Seals*, Collins, 1974

Neal, E G, *The Badger*, Collins, 1948, Pelican, 1958

Nethersole-Thompson, Desmond and Adam Watson, *The Cairngorms*, Collins, 1974

Perry, Richard, *Wildlife in Britain and Ireland*, Croom Helm, 1978

Ritchie, J, *The Influence of Man on Animal Life in Scotland*, Cambridge University Press, 1920

Shorten, Monica, *Squirrels*, Collins, 1954

Smith, M, *The British Amphibians and Reptiles*, Collins, 1951

Stephen, David, *Highland Animals*, Highlands and Islands Development Board, 1954

Stephen, David, *Watching Wildlife*, Collins, 1963

Thompson, H V and Worden A, *The Rabbit*, Collins, 1956

INDEX